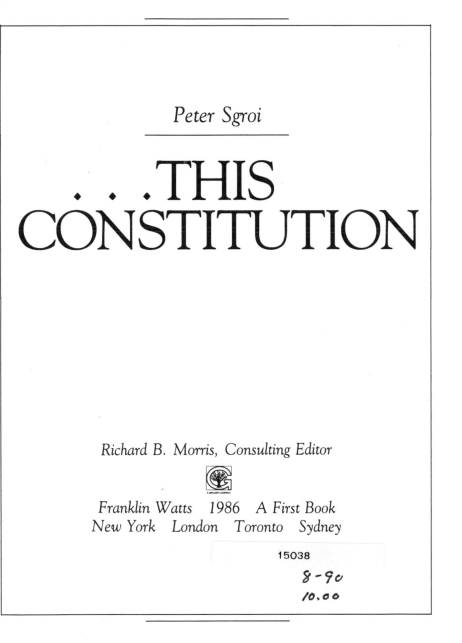

Peter Sgroi

. . . THIS CONSTITUTION

Richard B. Morris, Consulting Editor

Franklin Watts   1986   A First Book
New York   London   Toronto   Sydney

All photographs courtesy
of The Bettmann Archive.

Library of Congress Cataloging-in-Publication Data

Sgroi, Peter.
—this Constitution.

(A First book)
Bibliography: p.
Includes index.
Summary: Describes how the Constitution was written,
revised, approved, and enacted. Includes an outline
of its articles and amendments.
1. United States—Constitutional history—Juvenile
literature. [1. United States—Constitutional history]
I. Morris, Richard Brandon, 1904–   . II. Title.
KF4520.Z9S44   1986   342.73′029   85-31488
ISBN 0-531-10167-3   347.30229

Contents

. . . this Constitution

Acknowledgments

My thanks to my wife, Mary Anne, for
her patient help with the manuscript;
to the librarians Maureen Sullivan
and Norma Downer at Rye Neck High
School in Mamaroneck, New York, who
supplied excellent source material;
and to Carol Giarlo, who provided
indispensable secretarial assistance

Dedication

To Mariangelina and Dominick,
who had the courage to emigrate to America
as teenagers—my mother and father

Preface

While at the Constitutional Convention in Philadelphia during the summer of 1787, George Washington, the elected president of the group, realizing he might not get to his beloved Mount Vernon for the fall harvest, wrote home, "God only knows how long it will be after." Also he requested that his "blew coat with the cremson collar and his umbrella" be sent to him. He added that the honeysuckle against the house should be nailed up.

Washington's correspondence reminds us that the fifty-five delegates who attended the Constitutional Convention were not semidivine beings, but men. Truly they were the most talented men in America, but men nevertheless. Washington missed his home. At one point he had been away for six years leading the Continental Army through the successful American Revolution. Before Washington came to the Convention, his favorite brother had died and he suffered from an attack of rheumatism that was extremely painful.

Independence Hall in Philadelphia,
where the Constitutional Convention met in 1787

After the war, the national government had failed under the Articles of Confederation because of, among other things, the intense bickerings and jealousies among the states and the lack of corrective power to overcome both the domestic and international problems facing our young country. Ironically, the Philadelphia assemblage, although it was meeting to resolve some of the defects of the new government, continued to reflect these differences and rivalries.

During the seventeen long summer weeks and in the close confines of Independence Hall, the temperature outside many times matched the heated and fiery debates going on inside. Many delegates, because of illnesses in the family or extreme differences of opinions on various issues, departed the meeting and went home, never to return. About thirty of the fifty-five men representing twelve of the thirteen states (Rhode Island refused to participate) met daily and produced America's major document—". . . this Constitution."

In worrying about the fall harvest, little could George Washington have envisioned what he and his fellow delegates had sown that memorable summer of 1787. We are still today the receivers of this special harvest—two hundred years later.

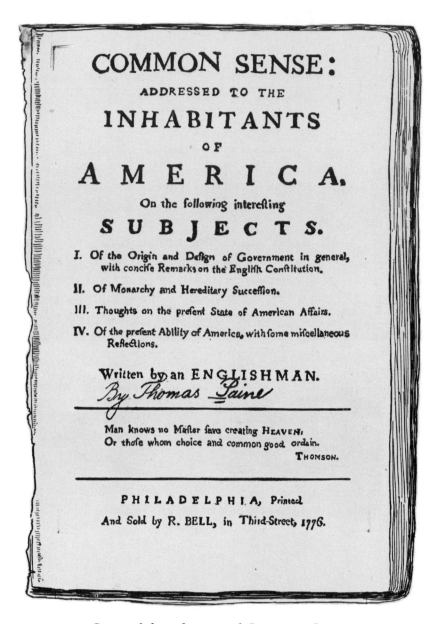

COMMON SENSE:

ADDRESSED TO THE

INHABITANTS

OF

AMERICA.

On the following interesting

SUBJECTS.

I. Of the Origin and Design of Government in general, with concise Remarks on the English Constitution.

II. Of Monarchy and Hereditary Succession.

III. Thoughts on the present State of American Affairs.

IV. Of the present Ability of America, with some miscellaneous Reflections.

Written by an ENGLISHMAN.

By Thomas Paine

Man knows no Master save creating HEAVEN,
Or those whom choice and common good ordain.
THOMSON.

PHILADELPHIA, Printed
And Sold by R. BELL, in Third-Street, 1776.

*Copy of the title page of Common Sense,
autographed by the author, Thomas Paine*

1

*Documents
of Freedom*

Common Sense

Thomas Paine, an English corset maker who came to the American colonies in 1774, sensed that "time hath found us." He wrote that a new era for governing had arrived and a new way of thinking was here. The Old World ways of the rich and upper class being superior and enjoying all the privileges of this world had to go. Why should they feel a race apart from the rest of mankind and the rest of us be forever destined to be illiterate, impoverished peasantry? This could no longer be tolerated by mankind.

He wrote this in a pamphlet called *Common Sense*, published in January 1776. Paine had a lot more to say in a bold way. He attacked King George III, the British ruler of the American colonies, as a royal brute. Paine felt strongly that kings and aristocratic ways were the natural enemies of human freedom. He felt people should never abandon their futures to an authority they cannot control. It didn't make any sense, he continued, that the tiny island of England should control the vast continent of North America. The American colonies had a moral obligation to become an independent nation, in fact a republic, a nation in which the power to govern is held by the citizens who elect representatives responsible to the people.

Before the publication of *Common Sense*, the colonies were already embattled with England. In spite of their differences, however, the thirteen colonies had not dreamed of separating from their mother country. This would be acting as traitors and "traitor" was an ugly word to the colonists. This attitude prevailed until several American minutemen were killed by the British at the Battle of Lexington on April 19, 1775.

When the Second Continental Congress assembled at Philadelphia in May, there were thousands of British regulars stationed there and more on the way. The Congress created a Continental Army and appointed George Washington commander in chief. As time went on, the Continental Congress acted more and more boldly. It began to allow privateers to raid British commerce, it opened hitherto closed American ports to foreign shipping, and it urged the colonies to create state governments.

The publication of *Common Sense* played a large part in helping the colonies break the strong thread of loyalty to the mother country. On January 31, 1776, Washington wrote, "The sound doctrine and unanswerable reasoning contained in the pamphlet *Common Sense* will not leave numbers at a loss to decide upon . . . separation." About 150,000 copies of the pamphlet were bought in the critical period from January to July 1776.

Lee's Resolution

John Adams of Massachusetts wrote, "by . . . every day Independence rolls in on us like a torrent." On June 7, 1776, Richard

Henry Lee of Virginia, a member of the Continental Congress, introduced a resolution of independence. In it he stated, "These United Colonies are and of right ought to be free and independent states, that they are absolved from all allegience to the British crown." In addition, he asked the colonies to review a plan for a national government and to seek foreign alliances.

The Congress discussed these ideas and agreed that before it voted on these points Thomas Jefferson of Virginia should lead a committee to draw up reasons for independence and John Dickinson of Delaware should head a committee to create a plan for a national government, or confederation, among the states. The colonies had reached the point of no return.

The Declaration of Independence

In addition to Thomas Jefferson, the committee that was selected to prepare a document justifying independence included Benjamin Franklin from Pennsylvania, Roger Sherman from Connecticut, Robert Livingston from New York, and John Adams from Massachusetts.

Thomas Jefferson, thirty-three, the youngest member of the Continental Congress, was selected to prepare the first rough copy. Jefferson wanted John Adams to do it, but Adams refused, saying, "You write ten times better than I can." The young Virginian understood that the underlying cause of the American Revolution included resentment of British trade regulations, which hampered colonial trade. He knew the colonists wanted self-government and should be taxed only by their own elected legislators. Taxation imposed by the British Parliament was taxation without representation. Illegal use of search warrants and the denial of trial by jury angered his countrymen. This was the denial of what they claimed "as rights of Englishmen."

Thirty-three-year-old Thomas Jefferson wrote the first draft of the Declaration of Independence in two weeks.

Jefferson explained he intended "to place before mankind the common sense of the subject, in terms so plain and firm as to command their assent. . . . It was intended to be an expression of the American mind."

He did this eloquently in his masterpiece, the Declaration of Independence, which took him two weeks to write. In this document he attacked the idea of the divine right of monarchs, that is, their claim that their right to rule came from God. Borrowing from eighteenth-century natural-rights philosophy, Jefferson wrote that the Creator granted all human beings certain rights that no government could take away. In fact, the reason government exists is to protect these rights of life, liberty, and the pursuit of happiness. Government, he further added, derives its just consent from the governed. He was describing the idea upon which the Americans were to base the creation of a new republican government. Jefferson then listed over two dozen examples of wrongdoings George III had inflicted on the colonies.

The final part of the document claimed the right of the colonies to be free and independent of Great Britain.

This rough copy, with a few changes made by Franklin and Adams, was officially adopted by the delegates of the Continental Congress on July 4, 1776. The following year this same body accepted the Articles of Confederation, a plan for a national government which was reported out of John Dickinson's committee. Out of necessity it was put into operation before all the states had ratified it. Congress was too busy at this time directing the war to debate this plan of federal union.

Chapter

2

Aftermath of
the Revolution

The last land battle of the American Revolution took place on November 10, 1782. George Rogers Clark and eleven hundred mounted riflemen took part in a battle near Chillicothe, Ohio. The peace treaty signed in 1783 was generous. The British conceded to the colonists all the land between the Allegheny Mountains and the Mississippi River in America. The northern boundary ran to the Great Lakes, and the southern boundary was declared between Spanish Florida and Georgia on the thirty-first north latitude. Fishing rights were given off the coast of Newfoundland and Gulf of St. Lawrence. But most important of all, Great Britain recognized the independence of the United States of America. A new nation was born!

The war, which lasted seven long years, left its physical marks. Norfolk, Virginia, for example, had been set aflame by the British and then again by the colonists themselves so the enemy could not use it. New York City had been partially destroyed by two fires. Few Americans were unaffected by the war. There were new widows and new orphans. Many Loyalists, those who believed in the crown, sadly left the United States in 1783. The total cost of the Revolution was estimated at between $104,000,000 and $135,000,000. Loans of $6,352,000, $248,000, and $1,304,000 to offset the cost were obtained from France, Spain, and Holland respectively. Repayment of these amounts added later on to the financial woes of the new nation.

Changes in America

The most important change resulting from the Revolutionary War was the creation of a separate and independent United States. Some historians believe the internal change from colony to state almost amounted to thirteen revolutions. As early as May 1776, the Second Continental Congress had urged each colony to draw up a state constitution. By war's end all had complied. The ease and speed with which this happened led Thomas Jefferson to remark: "The people seem to have laid aside monarchical and taken up the republican government with as much ease as would have attended their throwing off an old and putting on a new suit of clothes."

The new constitutions had many similar democratic features. Most had two-house legislatures with broadened powers. The colonists' experience with royal governors made them cautious in creating an office of governor for each state. So they limited the office's powers. In addition, qualifications for holding office were made higher than for voting. To run for office a person had to own property or pay some taxes. New Jersey went as far as allowing women to vote, provided they met the property requirement.

Some constitutions provided a bill of rights which included guarantees of religious freedom, trial by jury, freedom of press, and the right to life, liberty, and property. Americans had a knack for self-government and, because of strong loyalties to their locale, provided broad powers to their state governments. It was their belief this was needed in order to solve a wide variety of problems that would arise at the state level. The people had very little experience with national government. Their experiences with England made them fearful of a strong central government.

Other democratic changes in America included a strict separation of church and state in most states. This meant tax dollars could not be used to support religious institutions. A large share of the land owned by the crown was taken by the states in the name of the people. With the departure of Loyalists and royal governors from American soil went the things connected with aristocracy. Their land was divided among many patriots. The manors in the colony of New York alone comprised 2,500,000 acres (1,011,750 hectares) in 1769. In the breakup of these great manors, for example, James de Lancey's land was distributed among 275 persons and Roger Morris's among 250.

The strong desire for self-government produced the beginning of a demand for free public schools. Jefferson realized that the country expected to rely on the good sense of the common people, and therefore education became important.

Rhode Island, Massachusetts, and Pennsylvania freed their slaves before 1783. Freed black men in New Jersey were allowed to vote. Southerners in general maintained a strong proslavery position. The slave issue and others would eventually cause friction among the northern, southern, and western parts of our young country.

The social, economic, and political changes in the states made creation of a truly national government difficult. Union among all the states was necessary if the nation was to be strong. However, the colonies' taste of harsh rule and tyranny made them prefer to command their own destinies.

But how could America face the question of maintaining order, gaining the respect of foreign nations, and organizing the western lands in thirteen different ways? Jefferson, writing in a letter from Paris in 1785, was hoping for more cooperation among the states: "The interest of the states ought to be made joint in every possible instance, in order to cultivate the idea of our being one nation."

The Articles of Confederation

One year after independence was announced the necessity for a national government became obvious. John Dickinson, with a committee of thirteen, prepared the Articles of Confederation. The Articles were approved by Congress in 1777 but did not become the law of the land until all the western lands, originally claimed by the states, were turned over to the national government in 1781. The war was fought with no federal constitution; there was only an informal union, with the Continental Congress exercising the necessary powers.

The Articles in 1781 served as a federal constitution with authority over the whole country and economy. They provided for a "perpetual union" among the states. A Congress was established in which each state was to have one vote. There was a jointly shared treasury, and Congress was entrusted with the management of foreign affairs, war, and a national postal service. Congress could

Mr Cerisier, from his humble Servant
John Adams.

THE
CONSTITUTIONS
OF THE
SEVERAL INDEPENDENT STATES
OF
A M E R I C A ;
THE
Declaration of Independence ;
THE
ARTICLES OF CONFEDERATION
BETWEEN THE SAID STATES ;
THE
TREATIES between HIS MOST CHRISTIAN MAJESTY
and the UNITED STATES of AMERICA.

Publiſhed by order of Congreſs.

PHILLADEPHIA:
PRINTED BY FRANCIS BAILEY, IN MARKET-STREET.
M.DCC.LXXXI.

also borrow money, appoint naval officers, and try to deal with the Indians.

The Articles of Confederation lasted eight years and did permit the favorable peace talks which resulted in the Treaty of Paris in 1783. The giving up of the states' claims to the western lands enabled the passage of the Northwest Ordinance in 1787. It was another major achievement. This law established the pattern by which new states could enter the Union on an equal basis with the rest of the thirteen original states.

But almost immediately, due to their design and to ensuing domestic and foreign affairs, the Articles were doomed to failure. Basic to the document was the principle that the independence and authority of the states should be preserved. It was a "firm league of friendship," and it gave the federal government all the powers connected with war and peace—except the important one of taxation. The national government could ask for money but could receive it only with the approval of the state legislatures. The central government was not allowed to tax imports. It had the power to regulate trade and affairs with the Indians but not trade among the states. The national government and the states both could issue paper money, and this caused financial havoc.

There was no chief executive, or president, under the Articles for fear of the loss of power among the states. A one-house Con-

*Copy of the title page of a
collection of the most important
United States documents created
prior to the Constitution,
autographed by John Adams*

gress, with each state allowed one vote, would decide on major issues such as making war, borrowing money, or raising an army, and decisions required the agreement of nine of the thirteen states. The members of Congress were paid by the states, and they could be recalled at any time. Treaties made by the United States could be canceled by the actions of the states. America's first written constitution was feeble and doomed to ultimate failure, particularly when each state was given the power to veto or block any changes to the document. To fix what was wrong with the Articles or what was not working well was almost impossible. All thirteen states had to approve the change!

The Need for
a New Constitution

With the removal of Great Britain as the common enemy, the glue that held the states together dried up. The states became jealous of each other and quarreled, refusing to help each other. New York and New Hampshire farmers fought over their conflicting claims to Vermont. Maryland and Virginia argued over the navigation of the Potomac River. New York taxed firewood from Connecticut and farm produce from New Jersey. The states set up their own standards of measurements and passed laws that conflicted with other states' laws.

Requesting funds from the states in order to keep the national government running properly was, as Robert Morris, superintendent of finances, stated, "like preaching to the dead." In the years 1781 to 1783 Congress asked for $10,000,000. By June 1784 less than $1,500,000 had been paid. The only state to pay even 25 percent of its quota was South Carolina. Delaware, North Carolina, and Georgia paid nothing at all!

This weak and ineffective government inspired no respect in Europe. When some of the states closed their ports to British ships, England got revenge by refusing to allow the British West Indies to trade with America. Our ambassador to England, John Adams, in trying to make a more favorable trade agreement with England's foreign minister, was treated in a sneering and arrogant way. Jokingly, the foreign minister asked whether his country should make one trade agreement or thirteen.

Our new nation invited further trouble from Great Britain when it refused to honor the part of the Treaty of Paris dealing with the repayment of debts. These debts were owed the colonists who remained loyal to the crown during the Revolutionary War.

As a result of this violation, the British stationed their troops along our northern frontier area—Lake Champlain, Oswego, Niagara, and Detroit. They refused to leave and held on until 1796, and war over this issue was only narrowly avoided.

Thomas Jefferson, our minister to France, wrote home in despair after working hard but failing to get our whale oil and tobacco into French ports: "We are the lowest and most obscure of the whole diplomatic tribe."

The situation in the southwest resulted in unfriendly relations with Spain. In 1783 the Spanish gained East and West Florida and the next year limited American shipping on the lower Mississippi River. John Jay, our secretary for foreign affairs, was sent to negotiate the opening of the Mississippi River and infuriated the western farmers when he did not press Spain for the shipping rights on this important waterway. The Spaniards were also inciting the Creek and Seminole Indians against people in this area. One person wrote to Jay threatening that if all these matters were not handled satisfactorily, "the southwestern farmers would throw off their allegiance and look elsewhere for help." Reflecting on this matter,

George Washington exclaimed that the West stood "upon a pivot; the touch of a feather will turn them away."

Further Trouble

In 1785–1786 a severe depression increased economic hardship among the states, particularly along the frontier area, where money was scarce. Many of the poor and members of the debtor class, such as farmers, asked the state governments to issue more money, which would cause inflation, so they could pay off their obligations. One of the states hardest afflicted was Massachusetts. Boston dominated the state government and favored trade over agriculture. Bankers loaned the farmers money and, when they could not pay back their loans, took their land. Daniel Shays, a veteran of the Revolution, lived in the western part of the state. He and his followers first tried to prevent the courts from meeting. The Shaysites, as they were called, took the law into their own hands. When Shays and twelve hundred of his followers tried to attack the Springfield arsenal in 1786, they were met and routed by state militia units. A second battle followed in the beginning of 1787, with the same results. The rebellion collapsed and Shays fled to Vermont.

The affluent were shocked by these disorders. Their well-being and property were now threatened. George Washington was led to exclaim: "There are combustibles in every state which a spark might set fire to. I feel more than I could express for the disorders which have arisen. Good God! Who . . . could have predicted them?"

Shays' Rebellion pointed out that a stronger central government was needed to maintain order and to handle the economy in such a way as to avoid financial chaos.

*The state militia and volunteers had to
put down Shays' Rebellion, which was a serious
threat to the government of Massachusetts.*

The decline in Congress was reflected when some of its members chose to take state offices instead and some just stayed away rather than sit in a legislative body with no power. The entire Congress contained ninety-one members, but seldom were more than one quarter of them in session.

Things looked bleak for our nation until there was a call in 1786 for all the states to meet at Annapolis, Maryland, to discuss the foreign trade problem. Of the nine states invited, only five sent delegates and not much could be accomplished. What did come out of the meeting was the recommendation of the thirty-three-year-old New York delegate, Alexander Hamilton, that all states send delegates to a meeting to be held in May 1787 that would "render the constitution of the Federal Government adequate to the exigencies [demands] of the Union." Hamilton's suggestion was adopted by the Annapolis group, and Congress officially approved it.

Congress then asked all the states to send delegates to a convention at Philadelphia "for the sole and express purpose of revising the Articles of Confederation." It was a formal acknowledgement that the present government was not working properly.

Chapter

3

The Constitutional Convention Convenes

The Convention and Delegates

Some of America's greatest men gathered in Philadelphia to attend what the newspapers at the time announced as a "Grand Convention" or "Federal Convention." It was later called the Constitutional Convention. There was no limit on the number of delegates to be sent, but the quality of the people who attended rose after George Washington announced he would attend. His personal friend General Henry Knox persuaded the general to go. Bells chimed and artillery boomed as an honor guard greeted him upon his arrival. He was America's most respected Revolutionary War hero, and the people loved him.

A total of seventy-four delegates was named by state legislatures. Rhode Island was the only state to decline an invitation. Fifty-five delegates actually attended, and, in the end, thirty-nine signed the finished Constitution.

In addition to George Washington the Virginia delegation included James Madison, who later was called the Father of the Constitution. Next to Benjamin Franklin, he was probably the most intellectually prepared delegate present. Described as "no bigger than a piece of soap," Jemmy, as his friends called him, kept the best written record of what happened. The Virginia group also included the governor of the state, Edmund Randolph.

The state of Pennsylvania had among its eight-member group Benjamin Franklin and Gouverneur Morris. Franklin was ailing and did not have much to say at the Convention. However, his presence alone added great support to the gathering. Gouverneur Morris, on the other hand, was quite active, taking part in the debates on 173 occasions.

New York presented one of the most quarrelsome delegations. It contained representatives of different political minds and philosophies. John Lansing and Robert Yates believed in the preservation of states' rights and were very much opposed to any system whose object was "the consolidation of the United States into one government." The third delegate, Alexander Hamilton, was of another mind, believing in a strong national government. Lansing and Yates, because of their strong political beliefs, left the proceedings and did not return.

Other notable Americans present included Robert Morris, financial genius of the American Revolution; James Wilson, a signer of the Declaration of Independence; John Dickinson, who chaired the committee that drew up the Articles of Confederation; General Charles Cotesworth, educated at Oxford University; and William Paterson, who was attorney general of New Jersey and eventually became the spokesman for the smaller states of the Convention.

Of the fifty-five delegates chosen to attend, two were college presidents, three were professors, and twenty-six were college graduates (ten from Princeton). Twenty-eight had served in Congress, and nine were foreign born. There were three physicians, thirteen large-scale farmers, eight merchants, and twenty-nine lawyers. Fifteen delegates owned slaves.

The average age of the delegates was a little over forty-three. The oldest was Benjamin Franklin, at eighty-one, and Jonathan Dayton of New Jersey, the youngest, was twenty-six.

Thirty had seen action in the Revolution, eight had signed the Declaration of Independence, and six had signed the Articles of Confederation.

The fifty-five delegates indeed represented a wealth of talent and worldly experience in governmental and business affairs. Although they represented different ideas and sections of the country, there was a great deal of common ground. They had a mutual respect for law, a similar belief in the power of reason, and regard for the individual human being. Many believed in the ability to compromise, that is, to give up a little of what you believe in and accept some things you do not fully believe in. After all, the order given to each of them from their individual state legislatures was to strengthen the central government.

Not all of America's leaders were present. Thomas Jefferson and John Adams were both abroad serving as ambassadors. Sam Adams and Thomas Paine were also missing. Patrick Henry, although picked as a delegate, did not attend because he felt the Convention was planned to deprive the states of their authority.

Rules

The Convention opened its first meeting on May 25, 1787, at the Pennsylvania State House in Philadelphia. Today we call it In-

George Washington presiding at the Constitutional
Convention in Philadelphia in 1787

dependence Hall. Robert Morris, the delegate from Pennsylvania, nominated George Washington to be president of this Convention. He was elected by every single member. The general then took his place at the desk on the raised platform which was provided for the chairman. It was the same desk upon which the Declaration of Independence had been signed. Washington remained mostly silent throughout the next seventeen weeks. In his silence was his strength. He lent dignity to the meetings and helped keep them going. Most delegates knew he believed in a strong central government.

A few days later the rules were adopted. They were kept quite few and simple. It was decided that all decisions needed a majority, that is, a vote of one more than half of the states present. At least a majority of each delegation had to be present to qualify to cast its one vote for the state on any given issue.

The respect the members had for each other was demonstrated in this rule: "Every member rising to speak, shall address the President: and whilst he should be speaking none shall pass between them, or hold discourse with another, or read a book, pamphlet, paper printed or manuscript." In other words, they should be polite and listen attentively.

Another rule required secrecy. "Nothing spoken in the House be printed or otherwise published or communicated." The reason for this rule, although it seems unusual at first glance, was to help avoid possible misunderstandings the public might have over some of the debates. It made the delegates feel comfortable about what they might say. It also allowed them to change their minds without looking foolish to the people back home. So for over three months no one outside the hall knew what was going on at this gathering. The secrecy rule was respected outside the meeting place, although at times some members needed to·be reminded of it. On a particular occasion Benjamin Franklin was telling his dinner guests the fable of the two-headed snake which starved to death because it could not decide on which side of the tree to pass; he wanted then to proceed to tell what happened in a debate that day. His guests reminded him of the secrecy rule.

Another helpful rule was suggested by Young Spaight of North Carolina. It allowed the delegates to go back and review or even change any points already agreed upon. This allowed a change of heart on any matter.

Washington also protected what each member might say by ordering the secretary of the Convention, Major Jackson of South Carolina, to record only the motions made and the votes taken.

These rules reveal that although there were strong differences among the membership, most were nevertheless willing to yield for the good of the country. These were honorable men.

4

Two Plans and
a Compromise

The Virginia Plan

On May 29, Edmund Randolph, governor of Virginia, introduced a fifteen-point plan that was to occupy the focus of attention for the rest of the summer. The Virginia Plan, as it would be called, took two to three hours to present and called for a "national consolidation" rather than a league of thirteen states. This bold new plan was an attempt to overcome the defects of the Articles of Confederation, under which it was almost impossible to force states to obey the national government. The Virginia Plan provided for a national government that would operate at the level of the people rather than the states. To carry out this idea, Edmund Randolph spoke of a two-house national legislature. This would be the place where the laws of the country would be made.

An even more daring part of the Plan provided for a national executive whose office would enforce these laws. Today we call this office the presidency. It did not exist under the Articles of Confederation, nor did Randolph's idea for a federal court system.

Today the highest court under this federal court system is called the United States Supreme Court.

Under the Virginia Plan the members of the lower house of the legislature were to be elected directly by the people. This eventually became our present-day House of Representatives.

Selection of membership to our present United States Senate, or upper house, began with the idea that nominees would be selected by state legislatures and voted on by the House of Representatives. Eventually, through further debate, the delegates all agreed that the selection of senators would be made by state legislatures.

Members of both houses, it was suggested, would vote as individuals and not as state delegations with only one vote per state. The change would follow the practice of the Continental Congress rather than the method used under the Articles.

Each state was to have its number of representatives based on the size of its population. This Plan overwhelmingly favored the large states, such as Virginia and Pennsylvania, since they were more heavily populated than the smaller states, such as Delaware and New Jersey.

The Virginia Plan was put together in an earlier meeting of the entire Virginia delegation in which James Madison took a prominent part. Madison's biographers claim he drafted it. Madison himself said the plan was a "consultation among the deputies, the whole number seven being present."

The Plan certainly went beyond the original intent of the Convention—to revise the Articles of Confederation. In fact, it considered a remodeling of the entire national government!

The next step was to debate the Virginia Plan. The Convention did this by voting itself into a Committee of the Whole, as it was called, consisting of all its membership. The Committee of the Whole allowed members to speak freely, change their minds,

For the part he played in the Convention,
James Madison is often called the "Father
of the Constitution." He was thirty-six.

resubmit plans, and even vote without it counting or being recorded. George Washington was allowed to join the Virginia delegation, and the Committee of the Whole was run by Nathaniel Gorham of Massachusetts.

The first important vote came immediately. The Committee of the Whole voted yes to the point "that the national legislature ought to consist of two branches." Most state legislatures had two-house, or bicameral, legislatures and so agreement on this was easy, and, almost unaware the members had voted for dumping the Articles of Confederation for a new national government.

Most of them found comfort in the thought that however radical their Plan was, they were only putting together a proposal. Was it not the job of the states later to vote agreement or disagreement on the work created here in Philadelphia?

Who Was to Vote?

The question of who should vote for the members of the Senate and the House of Representatives produced heated arguments. Roger Sherman of Connecticut and Eldridge Gerry of Massachusetts both opposed popular elections, that is, the procedure whereby people vote directly for the legislators. They mistrusted democracy. Gerry felt that "all the evils we experience flow from the excess of democracy." He had not forgotten Shays' Rebellion, which took place in his state. Virginia's George Mason believed the people could be depended on and pleaded that representatives should be elected directly by the people. His point of view passed by a vote of six states to two with two states divided. The term of office for the membership of the House of Representatives was established later in the Convention at two years.

James Madison also wished the Senate to be elected by the people, but this time Eldridge Gerry's arguments won. It was decided that the state legislatures should elect the senators, who should have six-year terms. This was an indirect way. In this case the Philadelphia convention trusted elected officials more than the people themselves. It was not until the Seventeenth Amendment to the Constitution was passed in 1913 that United States senators were elected directly by the people.

And so the national legislative branch of government was proposed. It was called Congress rather than Parliament, as it is called in England, to keep the continuation of the name for the Continental Congress. This branch of government was to be responsible for creating our nation's laws.

The delegates postponed discussion of decisions to be made concerning the executive and the national courts, both of which were called for in the Virginia Plan. They did agree on the idea that there should be only a single executive.

Nathaniel Gorham, chairman of the Committee of the Whole, was about to present a report summarizing the points of agreement when something unexpected happened that almost caused the delegates to pack their bags and leave this historic session. William Paterson, delegate from New Jersey, who apparently reflected on what the Virginia Plan was really all about, introduced an alternative plan, which he called the New Jersey Plan. Paterson realized the delegates were not revising the Articles of Confederation but creating an entirely new government at the expense of the authority of the states. The larger states, he felt, were swallowing up the smaller ones, and he rallied to the smaller states' cause.

The New Jersey Plan

William Paterson, described as "one of those kind of men" who speaks only when he understands his subject well, spoke for the delegations who feared the creation of a strong central government.

He wanted to keep the Articles of Confederation and simply redesign them to eliminate their original flaws. He wished to keep a single legislative body which would get its power from the states and not the people. His one-house Congress would not be allowed to act on all national concerns—it would be limited. His New Jersey Plan also proposed the selection of more than one executive and made no provisions for a national court system.

It now came down to a fight between the small and the large states. The Committee of the Whole quickly rejected the New Jersey Plan on the first vote, and the Delaware delegate made a threatening attack on the large states. "The large states dare not dissolve to Confederation," he said. "If they do the small ones will find some foreign ally of more honor and good faith. . . ." Benjamin Franklin suggested that prayer should be introduced at the beginning of each session. Luther Martin of Maryland reported that the Convention was on the verge of breaking up, "scarce held together by the strength of a hair." Charles Cotesworth Pinckney suggested the Convention should adjourn for two days, and a "Grand Committee," represented by a member of each state's delegation, propose a solution. The advice was followed.

The compromise committee—led by Roger Sherman with help from his fellow Connecticut representatives, William Samuel Johnson and Oliver Ellsworth—proposed "the Great Compromise" to the Convention when it reassembled. It was the first of many to come, causing the Constitution to be called "a bundle of compromises."

The Great, or Connecticut, Compromise suggested a two-house legislature composed of a House of Representatives and a Senate. The number of each state's members in the House was to depend on the size of its population. The House members were to vote individually and not as state delegations. This was to satisfy the large-state followers of the Virginia Plan. To make small states and supporters of the New Jersey Plan happy, the states would have equal representation in the Senate. Each state would have two senators. The senators would also vote individually and not as a delegation.

After eleven days of debating, the Great Compromise was adopted by a vote of 5 to 4. The Convention fortunately continued.

5

The Executive Branch

The Presidency

The Virginia Plan called for a president. It took the Convention quite a while to say "president." They always referred to the office as the chief executive or the national executive. According to the Plan he was to be chosen by Congress and to serve for a term of four years. Along with some federal judges, the chief executive would have the right to veto the acts of Congress and review the laws of the states. In debating these proposals the issues raised became complex. How was the president to be elected—by direct popular vote? by Congress? by the state governors? or perhaps the state legislatures? When the length of his term came up, some suggested as few as three years, others as many as fifteen—and Alexander Hamilton proposed life! James Wilson of Pennsylvania recommended the people directly vote for the office, but this lost out because many of the delegates mistrusted the masses. The idea of more than one executive did not succeed either, but most did agree the president should be allowed to run for reelection. The

The first president, George Washington, with Henry Knox,
secretary of war; Alexander Hamilton, secretary of
the treasury; Thomas Jefferson, secretary of state; and
Edmund Randolph, attorney general

idea that Congress should elect the president was also dropped because everyone preferred a separation of the executive, legislative, and judicial branches. In fact, to make sure that no one branch became too powerful, the Convention established a "checks and balances system," whereby each branch watches and limits the power of the other two. The president, for example, would be able to veto a bill of Congress, and the Senate could block presidential treaty-making and appointments. The delegates probably assumed that the highest federal court—later to be called the Supreme Court—would decide if state or federal laws conflicted with the Constitution. This was never written into the document.

Electoral College

Instead of having the people elect the president directly, the Constitutional Convention considered having a special group of people called electors vote for the chief executive. They would be elected directly by the people. The large states liked this approach because it gave them an obvious advantage; however, it made the small states unhappy.

The question of electing the chief executive was turned over to a committee which devised a plan that won approval. Under this design each state was free to have presidential electors chosen either by the legislatures—as most of them did—or by popular vote. Now all electors are elected directly by the voters. The number of representatives and senators from each state would determine the number of electoral votes for each state. The electors voted for two candidates. The candidate who received the largest number of votes would be president, the second highest vote getter, the vice-president. The group of electors meeting to vote for the president and vice-president is called the Electoral College. Today electors state their choice for president and for vice-president.

If a presidential candidate did not receive a majority of the Electoral College vote, the House of Representatives voting by states would make the choice. This has happened in the elections of 1800 and 1824, when the House of Representatives chose Thomas Jefferson and John Quincy Adams. This method resolved the question of how to elect the president.

Powers of the President

The agreement that the office of the president should be a strong one was surprising. Perhaps the delegates' memory of the tyranny experienced under King George III was tempered by the fact that George Washington was everyone's choice when the office was created. His honesty and honor were beyond question.

So the delegates bestowed powers upon the presidential office along with some safeguards. The president was made commander in chief of the army and navy and of the state militias; he could make treaties with foreign powers, provided two-thirds of the Senate agreed. His choice of ambassadors, ministers, consuls, and judges of the federal courts required approval of the Senate. He could call special sessions of Congress. He was allowed to veto, or kill, congressional bills; however, a two-thirds vote of both houses could override his veto. Congress was also given the power to remove the president; he could be impeached by the House of Representatives and convicted of the charge by a two-thirds vote of the Senate. No president has ever been removed from office, although President Andrew Johnson was impeached in 1868 and missed being convicted by one vote!

The office of the presidency was given much power to meet emergencies, begin new programs, and focus debate on the important needs of the country. Yet, there were precautions taken to prevent the overstepping of his bounds.

Chapter

6

*The Convention
Finishes Its Work*

Overcoming the Defects

By creating the office of the presidency a major defect of the
Articles of Confederation was overcome. It is surprising how easily
other flaws were eliminated without much debate. A system of
United States courts, separate from the state courts, was established. The only court specifically mentioned was a Supreme Court,
leaving it up to Congress as to how many judges it should have
and the number of lower courts to be established.

Most of the delegates agreed that Congress should regulate
commerce, both among the states and with foreign nations. Only
one delegate voted against giving the national government the
power to tax. Many members of the Convention also voted to
forbid the states to issue paper money. It was well remembered
that these were the very reasons the Philadelphia convention was
held—the lack of control over interstate commerce and the inability of Congress to support the national government through

taxation. Even the amending process was made easier. The Convention believed that perhaps what they presently created was not so perfect and future circumstances and wiser heads would need to change what they created. So they improved the amending process—going from consent by all the states under the Articles to passage by Congress of the suggested change with approval by only three-quarters of the state legislatures.

A point was reached by July 26 wherby a review of what had been accomplished was in order. A Committee of Detail was selected under the chairmanship of John Rutledge of South Carolina to fulfill this task. The group adjourned for ten days.

By August 6 members received the fruit of their work—a seven-page pamphlet printed overnight by the firm of Dunlop and Claypoole in Philadelphia. It contained a preamble and twenty-three sections.

Each of these twenty-three parts was debated again although much of what was listed had already been accepted. It was at this point that the final compromises dealing with the so far undiscussed slavery issue as well as the commerce and tariff questions were reached.

Final Compromises

Madison warned the delegates that the real division of interest "did not lie between the large and small states; it lay between the northern and southern." The counting of people in each state for representation and tax purposes presented such a problem. The southerners wished to include their slaves in the count for representation but not in the count for tax purposes. The northerners believed the slaves should be counted for tax reasons and not representation.

The differences were settled by counting "free persons, those bound for service [indentured servants] excluding Indians and three-fifths of all other persons" for both taxes and representation.

Of course the "other persons" were the slaves. Five slaves were counted as three persons. This resolution of the problem became known as the "three-fifths" compromise.

Southerners also feared that the national government might put an end to slave trade. It was decided Congress could not prevent the importation of slaves until 1808. Congress could however impose a ten-dollar-a-head tax on each imported slave.

The northern and southern states also looked differently on the tariff question. A tariff is a tax on imported goods. It is used to raise revenue for the national government. It is also used to protect American industry by raising the prices of competitive imported goods. The North, where our "infant industries" were beginning, favored the protective-type tariff. The South saw it ruinous to its trade since it was mainly an agricultural, not an industrial, exporter. For them it only raised the price of imported goods.

The South also feared that giving the national government control over interstate and foreign commerce would work against its best interests. Southern fears were stilled through compromise again. Congress could control commerce and tariffs but with certain limits. A tariff was permitted only on imports and not on exports. A two-thirds vote was needed to ratify a treaty. The South figured

The South was reluctant to abolish slave trade, which was important to its economy.

it could block unfavorable trade treaties because at the time it controlled half the Senate votes.

During the debates over the "three-fifths" compromise, the question came up about how new states would be admitted into the Union and what role they should play in the new government. Gouverneur Morris, representing the rich, property-owning citizens, looked at the small western farmer as a lowly creature, unschooled and not very responsible. He thought the number of representatives chosen from the West should never be any more than the number chosen by the Atlantic states. Fortunately, the Convention followed the advice of his fellow delegate, James Wilson, who believed "if the interior country should acquire a majority" it has the right to make use of this situation. It was left up to Congress to determine the basis for admission of new states into the Union.

Many delegates mistakenly felt comforted by the thoughts of Roger Sherman. He gave expression to the idea that the future states would never go beyond the number of the existing states anyway.

The method of ratification of the Constitution—that is, the steps leading to approval of their work—had to be decided. Charles Pinckney, South Carolina's representative, earlier suggested and it was agreed that only nine states should be required to accept the document in order for it to become the Constitution of the United States. The delegates believed that not all the states would consent.

The next step agreed upon was to send a finished and signed copy of the Constitution to New York City, where the Continental Congress was meeting. From there copies of the document would be sent to the state legislatures. The state governments would then call ratifying conventions.

The Committee of Style
and Arrangement

Finally the debates ended. The work of one final committee was needed. This last committee included Gouverneur Morris, Rufus King, James Madison, William Samuel Johnson, and Alexander Hamilton. They were given the task of creating a polished, finished copy of the Constitution. The Committee of Style and Arrangement, as it was called, completed its task in two days. The Committee wrote a new introduction to the Constitution, called the Preamble, and reduced the twenty-three sections to seven. On September 10, 1787, the finished document was presented to the Convention; only two additional days were required for final agreement.

On September 17, the delegates gathered to sign the Constitution. Thirty-nine of the forty-one present did so. Edmund Randolph, whose Virginia Plan served as the basis for the new government, refused to sign. The long, hot summer's work—with sittings that lasted six and sometimes seven hours for more than four months—had come to an end.

After the closing of the session some members bade each other good-bye; others went to the City Tavern on Walnut Street for a farewell dinner. The next day the delegates headed home, bracing for the ratification fight. The state governments must now approve their work.

Chapter

7

The States Ratify
the Constitution

Arguments Against
the Constitution

In the contest for approval or disapproval of the Constitution an unanticipated situation developed. Political parties were formed almost naturally as citizens took sides on this issue. Today we accept without question major political parties, such as the Democratic and the Republican parties. We realize they organize and control our governments on a local, state, and national level by peaceful means. The people elect their candidates to government offices. Political parties grew out of the struggle over the Constitution in 1787.

Those who supported the Constitution were called Federalists and were led by such people as Alexander Hamilton, James Madison, and John Jay. Patrick Henry, Samuel Adams (who withdrew his objections when a Bill of Rights was added to the Constitution), and Richard Henry Lee led the opposing forces and were called

Anti-Federalists. They are the ancestors of our modern-day political parties.

There really was no clear set of differences. One party did not consist of just the wealthy, nor did one group trust the people more than did the other.

The Anti-Federalists were certainly not more democratic-minded than the Federalists. More than half of them were opposed to democracy, while someone like Alexander Hamilton, a Federalist, believed the people must be included if the government was to succeed.

A great deal of the hostility between the Federalists and the Anti-Federalists was personal. Edmund Randolph, Eldridge Gerry, and George Mason, all delegates to the Convention, did not sign the Constitution because some of their ideas had not been included in the document. Randolph, however, in the end supported the Constitution at the Virginia ratifying convention. Some of the wealthiest men, such as James Winthrop, who was from a very rich family in New England, opposed the Constitution. In Virginia some of the most established areas voted against the Constitution while frontier areas voted for it.

Anti-Federalists feared the creation of a strong central government. A great many of them believed, "that government is best which governs least." One excited opponent of the Constitution exclaimed: "The Constitution is a beast, dreadful and terrible which devours, breaks into pieces, and stamps the states with its feet!"

Although no clear division can be seen between the forces for and those opposed to ratification, it appears that those who earned a living by some form of commerce—merchants, shipowners, city craftsmen—were for the Constitution, while the people who had to make their living from the soil, the "dirt farmers," tended to oppose it.

Anti-Federalist arguments opposing the Constitution were: there are no guarantees of traditional rights for the individual, such as freedom of press, religion, assembly; state governments will be serving the national government; the president might become a dictator; only the rich will be able to hold office; debtors can no longer count on the value of paper money to repay loans; and tax collectors will be everywhere since the citizen will now be obligated to pay taxes to both the national and state governments.

Among the people, those opposed to the Constitution out-numbered those who favored it. If a popular election had been held instead of the state ratifying conventions, the Constitution would perhaps have been rejected.

Arguments for the Constitution

The Federalists argued that the Constitution was a good choice and it could well handle the present problems facing the nation. They reminded Americans of Shays' Rebellion. Many of them felt the new government would bring prosperity to a country which had suffered through a severe economic depression in 1785–1786. They pointed out that the new provisions for the central government were designed to deal with foreign nations and trade, as well as to control interstate commerce and currency.

The Federalists made much of the support given to the Constitution by George Washington and Benjamin Franklin. Their blessing was a major force in itself.

Benjamin Franklin was one of the most important founding fathers of the United States.

THE

FEDERALIST:

A COLLECTION

OF

E S S A Y S,

WRITTEN IN FAVOUR OF THE

NEW CONSTITUTION,

AS AGREED UPON BY THE FEDERAL CONVENTION,
SEPTEMBER 17, 1787.

IN TWO VOLUMES.

VOL. I.

N E W - Y O R K:

PRINTED AND SOLD BY J. AND A. M'LEAN,
No. 41, HANOVER-SQUARE,
M. DCC. LXXXVIII.

*Copy of the title page of one of two volumes
of* The Federalist, *a collection of essays that
supported the ratification of the Constitution*

The slogans of 1776 were out of date, explained the pro-Constitutionists, and the problem facing the nation was now not tyranny but the possible breakup of the nation. Certain powers, they continued to say, such as control of commerce, along with war and foreign affairs, must be national in scope.

In numerous articles to newspapers and in pamphlets, writers further argued that the states were not in danger of being taken over. They reminded everyone of the division of the central government into three branches—the executive, legislative, and judicial—a guarantee against abuse of power. They wrote that each branch was independent of each other and performed different functions of government. The legislative branch created the laws while the executive branch saw to their enforcement. The judicial branch was involved in settling differences in legal matters through the court system.

The branches also "checked and balanced" each other, acting as watchdogs making sure neither branch encroached on another's duties and responsibilities.

Perhaps the most convincing and best-written arguments were eighty-five articles, reprinted in many newspapers, composed by Alexander Hamilton, James Madison, and John Jay. *The Federalist Papers*, as they were to be called, brilliantly explained the defects of the Articles of Confederation as well as the benefits that the new government would provide the people. Even today these writings serve as the best explanation and support of the Constitution.

Federalists Are Better Organized

Although the Anti-Federalists wrote twice as much material against the Constitution, the Federalists were better organized. On September 28, 1787, when Congress asked the states to immediately hold conventions to vote for or against approval of the Constitution, the Federalists had more members in leadership positions in each of the states. In the election districts of the time the more recently settled frontier areas, which tended to be opposed, were not properly represented. No one polled the voters at this time. The only recorded vote was that of the elected state delegates, who voted 844 to 467 in favor of the Constitution. These delegates had been selected by no more than 160,000 adult males.

The Anti-Federalists were at a further disadvantage in that they had begun their study of the Constitution after it was written whereas many of the Federalist leaders were members of the Philadelphia convention, which had created it.

Wherever there was strong opposition, the pro-Constitution forces worked extra hard. In Pennyslvania, before the opposition could get to its feet, an election was held. In New York State, a two-thirds opposition in the state convention was converted through the persuasive efforts of Alexander Hamilton and John Jay.

The poor Anti-Federalists had nothing to offer but the weak Articles of Confederation. This led to their defeat.

Ratification

The ratification—voting for the Constitution—turned out to be a yearlong struggle. On December 7, 1787, Delaware became the first state to accept the Constitution. Within the next month, Pennsylvania, New Jersey, Georgia, and Connecticut also favored it. Like Delaware, New Jersey and Georgia both had no opposing votes, while Connecticut, led by Oliver Ellsworth and Roger Sherman, voted 128 to 40. In Pennsylvania two members of the assembly had to be dragged from their boarding houses to the statehouse in order to achieve enough votes to decide a date for a convention. Their final vote was 46 to 23.

A close battle followed in Massachusetts. At first it seemed the Anti-Federalists would have the upper hand. Then a mass meeting of Boston workmen brought opposition leader Sam Adams over to the other side. He was promised that certain changes to the Constitution would be made. These promises were carried out and are called amendments, or additions; the first ten became known as our Bill of Rights. It contains safeguards for individuals and states, such as freedom of press, religion, and assembly. Governor John Hancock changed his mind when he was promised support by the Federalists in the next election for governor and given a hint of their support for his achievement of high national office. Narrowly, Massachusetts voted 187 to 168 in favor.

Maryland and South Carolina voted in favor of the Constitution by large majorities, making them the seventh and eighth states—only one more was needed.

Big States Fall into Line

Upcoming were the battles for the big states. The Union could not survive without Virginia and New York. Virginia was the most populated state, and New York, situated between the North and South, was geographically vital.

George Washington, who supported the Constitution but did not attend the Virginia ratifying convention, sensed the drama when he wrote the Marquis de Lafayette: "The plot thickens fast. A few short weeks will determine the political fate of America."

The Anti-Federalist force included a prominent set of Virginia's leaders—Patrick Henry, George Mason, James Monroe,

John Tyler, and Richard Henry Lee. Even Thomas Jefferson, who was in France as our foreign minister, at first opposed ratification because he felt "one nation should not bind completely those to come." He concluded though, when he heard a Bill of Rights was to be added, that the rights of the people would be safeguarded. His change of heart and that of Edmund Randolph, the fine work of James Madison, and the impressive support of George Washington produced an 89 to 79 victory for the Federalists.

Defeat seemed almost certain in New York. Forty-six of the sixty-five delegates meeting at the Poughkeepsie convention were Anti-Federalists. Alexander Hamilton argued the states had nothing to fear from the new government. Most of the opposition centered outside New York City and was led by Governor George Clinton. Some Federalists argued that New York City might consider leaving the rest of the state and joining the Union by itself.

While the debates were going on, news came from New Hampshire. On June 21, 1788, the state had approved the Constitution 57 to 47. The Constitution was now in effect!

New York now had only the choice of being part of the country or not. The country needed New York, but New York also needed the country. For practical purposes, New York voted in favor by a close vote of 30 to 27.

It was another whole year before North Carolina voted in favor. At first it rejected ratification but when a Bill of Rights was promised, it changed its mind and on November 21, 1789, voted 195 to 77.

Under the threat to be left out of business relations with the United States, Rhode Island voted to approve. This state voted for the Constitution on May 29, 1790, by a vote of 34 to 32.

Church bells tolled, cannons boomed, as celebrations filled with emotions and rejoicing followed the acceptance of the new

At a parade in New York celebrating the ratification
of the Constitution, Washington returned the salute
of the Hamilton, *a float made up as a full-size frigate.*

form of government throughout the land. Parades and a holiday spirit became the order of the day.

At one such parade in Philadelphia on July 4, 1788, two floats in the parade summed up the story. One float displayed the Articles of Confederation as a flatboat which had crashed through the fault of a Captain Imbecile. It was poking fun at the defects of our first national government. The second float pictured the Constitution as a strong, firm ship ready to take to the high seas. It symbolized the hopes of all Americans.

On September 13, 1788, the Congress under the Articles of Confederation called for the first Congress under the new Constitution to meet on the first Wednesday in March 1789. The Articles were going out of business and the first president of the United States, George Washington, was about to be elected—with a new document to chart his course, the Constitution of the United States of America.

Chapter

8

Significance of
the Constitution

Today many people describe the worth of a product such as a car
in terms of its durability. How long has it been running? The
Constitution as the basic and supreme law of the land has been
running our country for two hundred years. Some of the fine tuning
and adjustments—the 462 additional words known as the Bill of
Rights—were made immediately. Some changes were made later,
such as the addition of sixteen more amendments. Thus this vehicle
of government, which sets down on the printed page the powers,
duties, and the form and structure of our government, was able to
weather such future storms as a Civil War, World War II, and the
Watergate scandal of the 1970s. It made provision for our vice-
president to temporarily take over the duties of president for just
eight hours under the Ronald Reagan administration in 1985.

The Constitution's simplicity of design has allowed it to be
interpreted in the light of contemporary circumstances and to be
constantly updated, particularly through Supreme Court decisions.

The "Constitution and Laws" are the bedrock on
which the liberty of Americans rests.

Chief Justice John Marshall explained it when he said the Constitution "was intended to endure for the ages . . . and consequently to be adapted to the various crises of human affairs." What those men created in Philadelphia was a living Constitution. It is a landmark in the age-old fight between tyranny and individual liberty, the "nice and exact adjustment of whose springs, wheels and weight," wrote John Adams, give insight into the inner workings of its power and limitations. It was crafted with self-regulating controls such as its "checks and balances" system. No one branch was allowed to overheat or become too powerful, and yet each held enough power together to run a country. In the process the states did not lose their identity and ability to deal with local problems. The Bill of Rights, the Constitution's first ten amendments, preserved our precious individuality. It did this by making it difficult for the federal government to take away rights such as freedom to worship, assemble, and have a free press. The Constitution protects the individual against the possibility of the abuse of power by the government. So successful has been this model that countries such as Canada, Mexico, Australia, France, Belgium, and Switzerland have adopted constitutions patterned in some degree after ours.

The significance of the Constitution also lies not only in what has been produced and endured but also in the process by which it was put together. Count Alexis de Tocqueville, a distinguished French visitor, wrote in 1833 of the emergence of the Constitution: "It is new in the history of society to see a great people turn a calm . . . eye upon itself when . . . the wheels of its government are stopped; to see it carefully examine the extent of the evil and patiently wait two whole years until a remedy is discovered, to which it voluntarily submits without costing a tear or a drop of blood from mankind."

The Constitution
of the United States

The Preamble states the purpose of the Constitution.

We the People of the United States, in Order to form a more perfect Union, establish Justice, insure domestic Tranquility, provide for the common defense, promote the general Welfare, and secure the Blessings of Liberty to ourselves and our Posterity, do ordain and establish this CONSTITUTION for the United States of America.

ARTICLE 1

Lawmaking powers are given to Congress.

SECTION 1. All legislative Powers herein granted shall be vested in a Congress of the United States, which shall consist of a Senate and House of Representatives.

How members of the HOUSE OF REPRESENTATIVES are to be chosen and serve

SECTION 2. The House of Representatives shall be composed of Members chosen every second Year by the People of the Several States, and the Electors in each State shall have the Qualifications requisite for Electors of the most numerous Branch of the State Legislature.

Who can be a representative

No Person shall be a Representative who shall not have attained to the Age of twenty-five Years, and been seven Years a Citizen of the United States, and who shall not, when elected, be an inhabitant of that State in which he shall be chosen.

How representatives and direct taxes are to be divided among the states

Representatives and direct Taxes shall be apportioned among the several States which may be included within this Union, according to their respective Numbers, which shall be determined by adding to the whole Number of free Persons, including those bound to Service for a Term of Years and excluding Indians not taxed, three fifths of all other Persons. The actual Enumeration shall be made within three Years after the first Meeting of the Congress of the United States, and within every subsequent Term of ten Years, in such Manner as they shall by Law direct. The Number of Representatives shall not exceed one for every thirty Thousand, but each State shall have at Least one Representative; and until such enumeration shall be made, the State of New Hampshire shall be entitled to chuse three, Massachusetts eight, Rhode Island and Providence Plantations one, Connecticut five, New York six, New Jersey four, Pennsylvania eight, Delaware one, Maryland six, Virginia ten, North Carolina five, South Carolina five, and Georgia three.

When vacancies happen in the Representation from any State, the Executive Authority thereof shall issue Writs of Election to fill such Vacancies.

Power to impeach officers of the executive or judiciary branch
How members of the SENATE *are to be chosen, and how they are to serve*

The House of Representatives shall chuse their Speaker and other Officers; and shall have the sole Power of Impeachment.

SECTION 3. The Senate of the United States shall be composed of two Senators from each State, chosen by the Legislature thereof, for six Years; and each Senator shall have one Vote.

Immediately after they shall be assembled in Consequence of the first Election, they shall be divided as equally as may be into three Classes. The Seats of the Senators of the first Class shall be vacated at the Expiration of the second Year, of the second Class at the Expiration of the fourth Year, and of the third Class at the Expiration of the sixth Year, so that one third may be chosen every second Year; and if Vacancies happen by Resignation, or otherwise, during the Recess of the Legislature of any State, the Executive thereof may make temporary Appointments until the next Meeting of the Legislature, which shall then fill such Vacancies.

Who can be a senator

No person shall be a Senator who shall not have attained to the Age of thirty Years, and been nine Years a Citizen of the United States, and who shall not, when elected, be an Inhabitant of that State for which he shall be chosen.

The Vice President of the United States shall be President of the Senate, but shall have no vote, unless they be equally divided.

The Senate shall chuse their other Officers, and also a President pro tempore, in the absence of the Vice President, or when he shall exercise the Office of President of the United States.

Power to try persons impeached by the House of Representatives

The Senate shall have the sole Power to try all Impeachments. When sitting for that purpose, they shall be on Oath or Affirmation. When the President of the United States is tried, the Chief Justice shall preside: And no person shall be convicted without the Concurrence of two thirds of the Members present.

Judgment in Cases of Impeachment shall not extend further than to removal from Office, and disqualification to hold and enjoy any Office of honor, Trust or Profit under the United States: but the Party convicted shall nevertheless be liable and subject to Indictment, Trial, Judgment and Punishment, according to Law.

Laws governing the holding of elections for representatives and senators, and when they shall meet

SECTION 4. The Times, Places and Manner of holding Elections for Senators and Representatives, shall be prescribed in each state by the Legislature thereof; but the Congress may at any time by Law make or alter such Regulations, except as to the Places of Chusing Senators.

The Congress shall assemble at least once in every Year, and such Meeting shall be on the first Monday in December, unless they shall by Law appoint a different Day.

SECTION 5. Each House shall be the Judge of the Elections, Returns and Qualifications of its own Members, and a Majority of each shall constitute a Quorum to do Business; but a smaller Number may adjourn from day to day, and may be authorized to compel the Attendance of absent Members, in such Manner, and under such Penalties as each House may provide.

Each House may determine the Rules of its Proceedings, punish its Members for disorderly Behaviour, and, with the Concurrence of two thirds, expel a Member.

Congress's house-keeping rules

Each House shall keep a Journal of its Proceedings, and from time to time publish the same, excepting such Parts as may in their Judgment require Secrecy; and the Yeas and Nays of the Members of either House on any question shall, at the Desire of one fifth of those Present, be entered on the Journal.

Neither House, during the Session of Congress,

shall, without the Consent of the other, adjourn for more than three days, nor to any other Place than that in which the two Houses shall be sitting.

SECTION 6. The Senators and Representatives shall receive a Compensation for their Services, to be ascertained by Law, and paid out of the Treasury of the United States. They shall in all Cases, except Treason, Felony, and Breach of the Peace, be privileged from Arrest during their Attendance at the Session of their respective Houses, and in going to and returning from the same; and for any Speech or Debate in either House, they shall not be questioned in any other Place.

Rights to salaries and immunities, and restrictions on holding other federal offices

No Senator or Representative shall, during the Time for which he was elected, be appointed to any civil Office under the Authority of the United States, which shall have been created, or the Emoluments whereof shall have been increased, during such time; and no Person holding any Office under the United States shall be a Member of either House during his continuance in Office.

SECTION 7. All Bills for raising Revenue shall originate in the House of Representatives; but the Senate may propose or concur with Amendments as on other bills.

Bills for raising money by taxes to originate in the House of Representatives, then be approved by the Senate

Every Bill which shall have passed the House of Representatives and the Senate, shall, before it becomes a Law, be presented to the President of the United States; If he approve he shall sign it, but if not he shall return it, with his Objections, to that House in which it shall have originated, who shall enter the Objections at large on their Journal, and proceed to reconsider it. If after such Reconsideration two thirds of that House shall agree to pass the bill, it shall be sent, together with the objections, to the

Any bill that is passed by both houses goes to the president. If he vetoes it (disapproves), it can become law only if both houses then pass it by two-thirds majority. Otherwise, the bill dies.

other House, by which it shall likewise be reconsidered, and if approved by two thirds of that House, it shall become a law. But in all such Cases the Votes of both Houses shall be determined by Yeas and Nays, and the Names of the Persons voting for and against the Bill shall be entered on the Journal of each House respectively. If any Bill shall not be returned by the President within ten Days (Sundays excepted) after it shall have been presented to him, the Same shall be a Law, in like Manner as if he had signed it, unless the Congress by their Adjournment prevent its Return, in which Case it shall not be a Law.

Every Order, Resolution, or Vote to which the Concurrence of the Senate and House of Representatives may be necessary (except on a question of Adjournment) shall be presented to the President of the United States; and before the Same shall take Effect, shall be approved by him, or being disapproved by him, shall be repassed by two thirds of the Senate and House of Representatives, according to the Rules and Limitations prescribed in the Case of a Bill.

SECTION 8. The Congress shall have Power To lay and collect Taxes, Duties, Imposts and Excises, to pay the Debts and provide for the common Defence and general Welfare of the United States; but all Duties, Imposts and Excises shall be uniform throughout the United States;

To borrow money on the credit of the United States;

To regulate Commerce with foreign Nations, and among the several States, and with the Indian Tribes;

To establish an uniform Rule of Naturalization, and uniform Laws on the subject of Bankruptcies thoughout the United States;

Powers given to Congress:

—to lay and collect taxes

—to borrow money

—to regulate commerce

—to establish rules for naturalization and bankruptcy

—to coin money

—to punish counterfeiting

—to create post offices

—to issue patents and copyrights

—to set up lower federal courts

—to punish piracies

—to declare war

—to create an army and a navy

—to call the militia

To coin Money, regulate the Value thereof, and of foreign Coin, and fix the Standard of Weights and Measures;

To provide for the Punishment of counterfeiting the Securities and current Coin of the United States;

To establish Post Offices and post Roads;

To promote the Progress of Science and useful Arts, by securing for limited Times to Authors and Inventors the exclusive Right to their respective Writings and Discoveries;

To constitute Tribunals inferior to the Supreme Court;

To define and punish Piracies and Felonies committed on the high Seas, and Offences against the Law of Nations;

To declare War, grant Letters of Marque and Reprisal, and make Rules concerning Captures on Land and Water;

To raise and support Armies, but no Appropriation of Money to that Use shall be for a longer Term than two Years;

To provide and maintain a Navy;

To make Rules for the Government and Regulation of the land and naval forces;

To provide for calling forth the Militia to execute the Laws of the Union, suppress Insurrections and repel Invasions;

To provide for organizing, arming, and disciplining the Militia, and for governing such Part of them as may be employed in the Service of the United States, reserving to the States respectively, the Appointment of the Officers, and the Authority of training the Militia according to the discipline prescribed by Congress;

To exercise exclusive Legislation in all Cases whatsoever, over such District (not exceeding ten

—to govern the District of Columbia

—to make "necessary and proper" laws needed to enforce these powers

Restrictions on the powers of Congress regarding:
—slave trade
—habeas corpus (appearance before a judge to determine if a person is being lawfully held)
—bill of attainder (declares person guilty without trial) and ex post facto law (passed after the crime was committed)
—tarriffs on exports

—preferential treatments for some states

Miles square) as may, by Cession of particular States, and the acceptance of Congress, become the Seat of the Government of the United States, and to exercise like Authority over all Places purchased by the Consent of the Legislature of the States in which the Same shall be, for the Erection of Forts, Magazines, Arsenals, dock-Yards, and other needful Buildings;—And

To make all Laws which shall be necessary and proper for carrying into execution the foregoing Powers, and all other Powers vested by this Constitution in the Government of the United States, or in any Department or Officer thereof.

SECTION 9. The Migration or Importation of such Persons as any of the States now existing shall think proper to admit, shall not be prohibited by the Congress prior to the Year one thousand eight hundred and eight, but a tax or duty may be imposed on such Importation, not exceeding ten dollars for each Person.

The Privilege of the Writ of Habeas Corpus shall not be suspended, unless when in Cases of Rebellion or invasion the public Safety may require it.

No Bill of Attaider or ex post facto Law shall be passed.

No capitation, or other direct, Tax shall be laid unless in Proportion to the Census or Enumeration herein before directed to be taken.

No Tax or Duty shall be laid on Articles exported from any State.

No Preference shall be given by any Regulation of Commerce or Revenue to the Ports of one State over those of another: nor shall Vessels bound to, or from, one State, be obliged to enter, clear, or pay Duties in another.

No Money shall be drawn from the Treasury, but in Consequence of Appropriations made by Law;

—*withdrawal of money from the Treasury*

—*titles of nobility and presents*

Restrictions of the powers of the states regarding:

—*making treaty or alliance*
—*issuing paper money*
—*keeping contracts from being carried out*
—*granting titles of nobility*
—*levying taxes on imports or exports*
—*keeping troops or ships of war in times of peace*
—*going to war without the consent of Congress*

Executive power given to the PRESIDENT

and a regular Statement and Account of the Receipts and Expenditures of all public Money shall be published from time to time.

No Title of Nobility shall be granted by the United States: And no Person holding any Office of Profit or Trust under them, shall, without the Consent of the Congress, accept of any present, Emolument, Office, or Title, of any kind whatever, from any King, Prince, or foreign State.

SECTION 10. No State shall enter into any Treaty, Alliance, or Confederation; grant Letters of Marque and Reprisal; coin Money; emit Bills of Credit; make any Thing but gold and silver Coin a Tender in Payment of Debts; pass any Bill of Attainder, ex post facto Law, or Law impairing the Obligation of Contracts, or grant any Title of Nobility.

No State shall, without the Consent of the Congress, lay any Imposts or Duties on Imports or Exports, except what may be absolutely necessary for executing its inspection Laws: and the net Produce of all Duties and Imposts, laid by any State on Imports or Exports, shall be for the Use of the Treasury of the United States; and all such Laws shall be subject to the Revision and Controul of the Congress.

No State shall, without the Consent of Congress, lay any duty of Tonnage, keep Troops, or Ships of War in time of Peace, enter into any Agreement or Compact with another State, or with a foreign Power, or engage in War, unless actually invaded, or in such imminent Danger as will not admit of delay.

ARTICLE II

SECTION 1. The executive Power shall be vested in a President of the United States of America. He shall hold his Office during the Term of four years, and, together with the Vice President, chosen for the same Term, be elected, as follows:

Each State shall appoint, in such Manner as the Legislature thereof may direct, a Number of Electors, equal to the whole Number of Senators and Representatives to which the State may be entitled in the Congress: but no Senator or Representative, or person holding an Office of Trust or Profit under the United States, shall be appointed an Elector.

The Electors shall meet in their respective States, and vote by Ballot for two Persons, of whom one at least shall not be an Inhabitant of the same State with themselves. And they shall make a List of all the Persons voted for, and of the Number of Votes for each; which List they shall sign and certify, and transmit sealed to the Seat of the Government of the United States, directed to the President of the Senate. The President of the Senate shall, in the Presence of the Senate and House of Representatives, open all the Certificates, and the Votes shall then be counted. The Person having the greatest Number of Votes shall be the President, if such Number be a Majority of the whole Number of Electors appointed; and if there be more than one who have such Majority, and have an equal Number of Votes, then the House of Representatives shall immediately chuse by Ballot one of them for President; and if no Person have a Majority, then from the five highest on the List the said House shall in like Manner chuse the President. But in chusing the President, the Votes shall be taken by States, the Representation from each State having one Vote; a quorum for this Purpose shall consist of a Member or Members from two thirds of the States, and a Majority of all the States shall be necessary to a Choice. In every Case, after the Choice of the President, the

How the president and VICE PRESIDENT *are to be chosen*

Person having the greatest Number of Votes of the Electors shall be the Vice President. But if there should remain two or more who have equal votes, the Senate shall chuse from them by Ballot the Vice President.

The Congress may determine the Time of chusing the Electors, and the Day on which they shall give their Votes; which Day shall be the same throughout the United States.

Who can be president

No person except a natural born Citizen, or a Citizen of the United States, at the time of the Adoption of this Constitution, shall be eligible to the Office of President; neither shall any Person be eligible to that Office who shall not have attained to the Age of thirty five years, and been fourteen Years a Resident within the United States.

Vice president becomes president if president is removed or dies.

In Case of the Removal of the President from Office, or of his Death, Resignation, or Inability to discharge the Powers and Duties of the said Office, the same shall devolve on the Vice President, and the Congress may by Law provide for the Case of Removal, Death, Resignation, or Inability, both of the President and Vice President, declaring what Officer shall then act as president, and such officer shall act accordingly, until the disability be removed, or a President shall be elected.

President's pay

The president shall, at stated Times, receive for his Services, a Compensation, which shall neither be increased nor diminished during the Period for which he shall have been elected, and he shall not receive within that Period any other Emolument from the United States, or any of them.

President's oath of office

Before he enter on the execution of his Office, he shall take the following Oath or Affirmation:—"I do solemnly swear (or affirm) that I will faithfully execute the Office of President of the United States,

Powers given to the president:

—be commander in chief of the armed forces
—grant pardons

—make treaties and appointments

Duties of the president:

—communicate to Congress

and will to the best of my Ability, preserve, protect and defend the Constitution of the United States."

SECTION 2. The President shall be Commander in Chief of the Army and Navy of the United States, and of the Militia of the several States, when called into the actual Service of the United States; he may require the Opinion, in writing, of the principal Officer in each of the executive Departments, upon any subject relating to the Duties of their respective Offices, and he shall have Power to Grant Reprieves and Pardons for Offences against the United States, except in Cases of Impeachment.

He shall have Power, by and with the Advice and Consent of the Senate, to make Treaties, provided two thirds of the Senators present concur; and he shall nominate, and by and with the Advice and Consent of the Senate, shall appoint Ambassadors, other public Ministers and Consuls, Judges of the supreme Court, and all other Officers of the United States, whose Appointments are not herein otherwise provided for, and which shall be established by Law: but the Congress may by Law vest the Appointments of such inferior Officers, as they think proper, in the President alone, in the Courts of Law, or in the Heads of Departments.

The President shall have Power to fill up all Vacancies that may happen during the Recess of the Senate, by granting Commissions which shall expire at the End of their next Session.

SECTION 3. He shall from time to time give to the Congress Information of the State of the Union, and recommend to their Consideration such Measures as he shall judge necessary and expedient; he may, on extraordinary occasions, convene both Houses, or either of them, and in Case of Disagreement between

—convene or adjourn Congress, in case of disagreement
—receive ambassadors
—execute laws
—commission officers

How president and other United States officers can be removed from office

Judicial power given to the SUPREME COURT and lower courts

Federal judges hold office for life "during good Behaviour."

The courts hear cases between states, between a state and a citizen of another state, between citizens of different states, and between a state or citizen and a foreign state or a foreign citizen. They also try cases arising from matters on the high seas.

them, with respect of them, and in Case of Disagreement between them, with respect to the Time of Adjournment, he may adjourn them to such Time as he shall think proper; he shall receive Ambassadors and other public Ministers; he shall take Care that the laws be faithfully executed, and shall Commission all the Officers of the United States.

SECTION 4. The President, Vice President and all civil Officers of the United States, shall be removed from Office on Impeachment for, and Conviction of, Treason, Bribery, or other high Crimes and Misdemeanors.

ARTICLE III

SECTION 1. The judicial Power of the United States, shall be vested in one supreme Court, and in such inferior Courts as the Congress may from time to time ordain and establish. The Judges, both of the supreme and inferior Courts, shall hold their Offices during good Behaviour, and shall, at stated Times, receive for their Services, a compensation, which shall not be diminished during their Continuance in Office.

SECTION 2. The judicial Power shall extend to all Cases, in Law and Equity, arising under this Constitution, the Laws of the United States, and Treaties made, or which shall be made, under their Authority;—to all Cases affecting Ambassdors, other public Ministers and Consuls;—to all cases of admiralty and maritime Jurisdiction;—to Controversies to which the United States shall be a Party;—to Controversies between two or more States;—between a State and Citizens of another State;—between Citizens of different States,—between Citizens of the same State claiming Lands under Grants of different States, and between a State, or the Citizens thereof, and foreign States, Citizens or Subjects.

In all Cases affecting Ambassadors, other public Ministers and Consuls, and those in which a State shall be Party, the supreme Court shall have original Jurisdiction. In all the other Cases before mentioned, the supreme Court shall have appellate Jurisdiction, both as to Law and Fact, with such Exceptions, and under such Regulations as the Congress shall make.

Anyone accused of a federal crime has the right to a trial by jury.

The trial of all Crimes, except in Cases of Impeachment, shall be by Jury; and such Trial shall be held in the State where the said Crimes shall have been committed; but when not committed within any State, the Trial shall be at such Place or Places as the Congress may be Law have directed.

Definition of, proof of, and punishment of treason

SECTION 3. Treason against the United States, shall consist only in levying War against them, or in adhering to their Enemies, giving them Aid and Comfort. No Person shall be convicted of Treason unless on the Testimony of two Witnesses to the same overt Act, or on Confession in open Court.

The Congress shall have power to declare the Punishment of Treason, but no Attainder of Treason shall work Corruption of Blood, or Forfeiture except during the Life of the person attainted.

ARTICLE IV

Respect by other states of each other's laws, records, and court decisions

SECTION 1. Full Faith and Credit shall be given in each State to the public Acts, Records, and judicial Proceedings of every other State. And the Congress may by general Laws prescribe the Manner in which such Acts, Records and Proceedings shall be proved, and the Effect thereof.

Each state to welcome citizens from other states

SECTION 2. The Citizens of each State shall be entitled to all Privileges and Immunities of Citizens in the several States.

A Person charged in any State with Treason, Felony, or other Crime, who shall flee from Justice,

Obligation to return fleeing criminals or slaves

and be found in another State, shall on demand of the executive Authority of the State from which he fled, be delivered up, to be removed to the State having Jurisdiction of the crime.

No Person held to Service or Labour in one State, under the Laws thereof, escaping into another, shall, in Consequence of any Law or Regulation therein, be discharged from such Service or Labour, but shall be delivered up on Claim of the Party to whom such Service or Labour may be due.

Power of Congress over creation of new states and over territory and other property

SECTION 3. New States may be admitted by the Congress into this Union; but no new State shall be formed or erected within the Jurisdiction of any other State; nor any State be formed by the Junction of two or more States, or parts of States, without the Consent of the Legislatures of the States concerned as well as of the Congress.

The Congress shall have power to dispose of and make all needful Rules and Regulations respecting the Territory or other Property belonging to the United States; and nothing in this Constitution shall be so construed as to Prejudice any Claims of the United States, or of any particular State.

Each state guaranteed a republican form of government and protection

SECTION 4. The United States shall guarantee to every State in this Union a Republican Form of Government, and shall protect each of them against Invasion; and on Application of the Legislature, or the Executive (when the Legislature cannot be convened) against domestic Violence.

ARTICLE V

To change or amend the Constitution:

The Congress, whenever two thirds of both Houses shall deem it necessary, shall propose Amendments to this Constitution, or, on the Application of the Legislatures of two thirds of the several States,

(1) Congress by a two-thirds vote or a convention called by two-thirds of the states can propose amendment.

(2) Three-fourths of the state legislatures must approve it.

shall call a Convention for proposing Amendments, which, in either Case, shall be valid to all Intents and Purposes, as part of this Constitution, when ratified by the Legislatures of three fourths of the several States, or by Conventions in three fourths thereof, as the one or the other Mode of Ratification may be proposed by the Congress; Provided that no Amendment which may be made prior to the Year One thousand eight hundred and eight shall in any Manner affect the first and fourth Clauses in the Ninth Section of the First Article; and that no State, without its Consent, shall be deprived of its equal Suffrage in the Senate.

ARTICLE VI

All obligations made before the adoption of the Constitution to be honored

All Debts contracted and Engagements entered into, before the Adoption of this Constitution, shall be as valid against the United States under this Constitution, as under the Confederation.

"This Constitution" and the laws of the United States are the supreme law of the land.

This Constitution, and the Laws of the United States which shall be made in Pursuance thereof; and all Treaties made, or which shall be made, under the Authority of the United States, shall be the supreme Law of the Land; and the Judges in every State shall be bound thereby, any Thing in the Constitution or Laws of any State to the Contrary notwithstanding.

Pledge required of all officials to support the Constitution, but no religious test can ever be required

The Senators and Representatives before mentioned, and the Members of the several State Legislatures, and all executive and judicial Officers, both of the United States and of the several States, shall be bound by Oath or Affirmation to support this Constitution; but no religious Test shall ever be required as a qualification to any Office or public Trust under the United States.

ARTICLE VII

The Ratification of the Conventions of nine States shall be sufficient for the Establishment of this Constitution between the States so ratifying the same.

Done in Convention by the Unanimous Consent of the States present the Seventeenth Day of September in the Year of our Lord one thousand seven hundred and Eighty seven, and of the Independence of the United States of America the Twelfth. In Witness whereof We have hereunto subscribed our names.

Articles in Addition to, and Amendment of, the Constitution of the United States of America. Proposed by Congress, and Ratified by the Legislatures of the Several States, Pursuant to the Fifth Article of the Original Constitution.

AMENDMENT I [1791]

Congress shall make no law respecting an establishment of religion, or prohibiting the free exercise thereof; or abridging the freedom of speech, or of the press; or the right of the people peaceably to assemble, and to petition the Government for a redress of grievances.

AMENDMENT II [1791]

A well regulated Militia, being necessary to the security of a free State, the right of the people to keep and bear Arms shall not be infringed.

AMENDMENT III [1791]

No Soldier shall, in time of peace, be quartered in any house, without the consent of the Owner, nor in time of war, but in a manner to be prescribed by law.

AMENDMENT IV [1791]

*Prohibition of unrea-
sonable search and
seizures*

The right of the people to be secure in their persons, houses, papers, and effects, against unreasonable searches and seizures, shall not be violated, and no Warrants shall issue, but upon probable cause, support by Oath or affirmation, and particularly describing the place to be searched, and the persons or things to be seized.

AMENDMENT V [1791]

*Rights of accused
persons*

No person shall be held to answer for a capital, or otherwise infamous crime, unless on a presentment or indictment of a Grand Jury, except in cases arising in the land or naval forces, or in the Militia, when in actual service in time of war or public danger; nor shall any person be subject for the same offence to be twice put in jeopardy of life or limb; nor shall be compelled in any criminal case to be a witness against himself, nor be deprived of life, liberty, or property, without due process of law; nor shall private property be taken for public use, without just compensation.

AMENDMENT VI [1791]

*Right to a speedy,
fair trial*

In all criminal prosecutions, the accused shall enjoy the right to a speedy and public trial, by an impartial jury of the State and district wherein the crime shall have been committed, which district shall have been previously ascertained by law, and to be informed of the nature and cause of the accusation; to be confronted with the witnesses against him; to have compulsory process for obtaining witnesses in his favor, and to have the Assistance of Counsel for his defence.

AMENDMENT VII [1791]

In suits at common law, where the value in controversy shall exceed twenty dollars, the right of trial by

Right of trial by jury

jury shall be preserved, and no fact tried by a jury, shall be otherwise reexamined in any Court of the United States, than according to the rules of the common law.

Prohibits excessive bail, fines, and "cruel and unusual" punishment

AMENDMENT VIII [1791]

Excessive bail shall not be required, nor excessive fines imposed, nor cruel and unusual punishments inflicted.

Rights listed in Constitution not the only rights that exist

AMENDMENT IX [1791]

The enumeration in the Constitution, of certain rights, shall not be construed to deny or disparage others retained by the people.

Powers not given to federal government belong "to the States . . . or to the people".

AMENDMENT X [1791]

The powers not delegated to the United States by the Constitution, nor prohibited by it to the States, are reserved to the States respectively, or to the people.

Limits on suits against states

AMENDMENT XI [1798]

The Judicial power of the United States shall not be construed to extend to any suit in law or equity, commenced or prosecuted against one of the United States by Citizens of another State, or by Citizens or Subjects of any Foreign State.

AMENDMENT XII [1804]

The Electors shall meet in their respective States, and vote by ballot for President and Vice-President, one of whom, at least, shall not be an inhabitant of

Manner of choosing president and vice president: Electoral college procedure revised

the same State with themselves; they shall name in their ballots the person voted for as President, and in distinct ballots the person voted for as Vice-President, and they shall make distinct lists of all persons voted for as President, and of all persons voted for as Vice-President, and of the number of votes for each, which lists they shall sign and certify, and transmit sealed to the seat of the government of the United States, directed to the President of the Senate;—The President of the Senate shall, in the presence of the Senate and House of Representatives, open all the certificates and the votes shall then be counted;— The person having the greatest number of votes for President, shall be the President, if such number be a majority of the whole number of Electors appointed; and if no person have such majority, then from the persons having the highest numbers not exceeding three on the list of those voted for as President, the House of Representatives shall choose immediately, by ballot, the president. But in choosing the president, the votes shall be taken by states, the representation from each state having one vote; a quorum for this purpose shall consist of a member or members from two-thirds of the states, and a majority of all the states shall be necessary to a choice. And if the House of Representatives shall not choose a President whenever the right of choice shall devolve upon them, before the fourth day of March next following, then the Vice-President shall act as President, as in the case of the death or other constitutional disability of the President.—The person having the greatest number of votes as Vice-President, shall be the Vice-President, if such number be a majority of the whole number of Electors appointed, and if no person have a majority, then from the two highest numbers on the list, the Senate shall choose the Vice-President; a quorum for the purpose shall consist of two-thirds of the whole number of Senators, and a majority of the whole number shall be necessary to a choice. But no person constitutionally ineligible to the office of President shall be eligible to that of Vice-President of the United States.

AMENDMENT XIII [1865]

Slavery abolished

SECTION 1. Neither slavery nor involuntary servitude, except as a punishment for crime whereof the party shall have been duly convicted, shall exist within the United States, or any place subject to their jurisdiction.

SECTION 2. Congress shall have power to enforce this article by appropriate legislation.

AMENDMENT XIV [1868]

Defines citizenship, and denies states right to deprive anyone of "due process of law" and "equal protection"

SECTION 1. All persons born or naturalized in the United States, and subject to the jurisdiction thereof, are citizens of the United States and of the State wherein they reside. No State shall make or enforce any law which shall abridge the privileges or immunities of citizens of the United States; nor shall any State deprive any person of life, liberty, or property, without due process of law; nor deny to any person within its jurisdiction the equal protection of the laws.

SECTION 2. Representatives shall be apportioned among the several States according to their respective numbers, counting the whole number of persons in each State, excluding Indians not taxed. But when the right to vote at any election for the choice of electors for President and Vice-President of

Declares every man over age of 21 to be entitled to one vote

the United States, Representatives in Congress, the Executive and Judicial officers of a State, or the members of the Legislature thereof, is denied to any of the male inhabitants of such State, being twenty-one years of age, and citizens of the United States, or in any way abridged, except for partcipation in rebellion, or other crime, the basis of representation therein shall be reduced in the proportion which the number of such male citizens shall bear to the whole number of male citizens twenty-one years of age in such State.

SECTION 3. No person shall be a Senator or Representative in Congress, or elector of President and Vice-President, or hold any office, civil or military, under the United States, or under any State, who, having previously taken an oath, as a member of Congress, or as an officer of the United States, or as a member of any State legislature, or as an executive or judicial officer of any State, to support the Constitution of the United States, shall have engaged in insurrection or rebellion against the same, or given aid or comfort to the enemies thereof. But Congress may by a vote of two-thirds of each House, remove such disability.

Southern rebels denied the right to hold federal office

SECTION 4. The validity of the public debt of the United States, authorized by law, including debts incurred for payment of pensions and bounties for services in suppressing insurrection or rebellion, shall not be questioned. But neither the United States nor any State shall assume or pay any debt or obligation incurred in aid of inurrection or rebellion against the United States or any claim for the loss of emancipation of any slave; but all such debts, obligations, and claims shall be held illegal and void.

Union war debts to be paid, but debts of the South declared "illegal and void"

SECTION 5. The Congress shall have power to enforce, by appropriate legislation, the provisions of this article.

AMENDMENT XV [1870]

Race no bar to voting rights

SECTION 1. The right of citizens of the United States to vote shall not be denied or abridged by the United States or by any State on account of race, color, or previous condition of servitude—

SECTION 2. The Congress shall have power to enforce this article by appropriate legislation.

AMENDMENT XVI [1913]

Authorizes individual federal income tax

The Congress shall have power to lay and collect taxes on incomes, from whatever source derived, without apportionment among the several States, and without regard to any census or enumeration.

AMENDMENT XVII [1913]

The Senate of the United States shall be composed of two Senators from each State, elected by the people thereof, for six years; and each Senator shall have one vote. The elecctors in each State shall have the qualifications requisite for electors of the most numerous branch of the State legislature.

United States senators to be elected directly by the people

When vacancies happen in the representation of any State in the Senate, the executive authority of such State shall issue writs of election to fill such vacancies: *Provided*, That the legislature of any State may empower the executive thereof to make temporary appointments until the people fill the vacancies by election as the legislature may direct.

This amendment shall not be so construed as to affect the election or term of any Senator chosen before it becomes valid as part of the Constitution.

AMENDMENT XVIII [1919]

SECTION 1. After one year from the ratification of this article the manufacture, sale, or transportation

Prohibits the manu-
facture, sale, and
shipment of alcoholic
beverages

of intoxicating liquors within, the importation thereof into, or the exportation thereof from the United States and all territory subject to the jurisdiction thereof for beverage purposes is hereby prohibited.

SECTION 2. The Congress and the several States shall have concurrent power to enforce this article by appropriate legislation.

SECTION 3. This article shall be inoperative unless it shall have been ratified as an amendment to the Constitution by the legislatures of the several States, as provided in the Constitution, within seven years from the date of the submission hereof to the States by Congress.

AMENDMENT XIX [1920]

Gives women the
right to vote

The right of citizens of the United States to vote shall not be denied or abridged by the United States or by any State on account of sex.

Congress shall have power to enforce this article by appropriate legislation.

AMENDMENT XX [1933]

President and vice
president to begin
terms on January 20,
members of Congress
on January 3

SECTION 1. The terms of the President and Vice-President shall end at noon on the 20th day of January, and the terms of Senators and Representatives at noon on the 3rd day of January, of the years in which such terms would have ended if this article had not been ratified; and the terms of their successors shall then begin.

SECTION 2. The Congress shall assemble at least once in every year, and such meeting shall begin at noon on the 3rd day of January, unless they shall by law appoint a different day.

SECTION 3. If, at the time fixed by the beginning of the term of the President, the President elect shall have died, the Vice-President elect shall become President. If a President shall not have been chosen before the time fixed for the beginning of his term, or if the President elect shall have failed to qualify, then the Vice-President-elect shall act as President until a President shall have qualified; and the Congress may by law provide for the case wherein neither a President elect nor a Vice-President elect shall have qualified, declaring who shall then act as President, or the manner in which one who is to act shall be selected, and such person shall act accordingly until a President or Vice-President shall have qualified.

Provides for emergency presidential succession

SECTION 4. The Congress may by law provide for the case of the death of any of the persons from whom the House of Representatives may choose a President whenever the right of choice shall have devolved upon them, and for the case of the death of any of the persons from whom the Senate may choose a Vice-President whenever the right of choice shall have devolved upon them.

SECTION 5. Sections 1 and 2 shall take effect on the 15th day of October following the ratification of this article.

SECTION 6. This article shall be inoperative unless it shall have been ratified as an amendment to the Constitution by the legislatures of three-fourths of the several States within seven years from the date of its submission.

AMENDMENT XXI [1933]

Repeals the eighteenth amendment

SECTION 1. The eighteenth article of amendment to the Constitution of the United States is hereby repealed.

SECTION 2. The transportation or importation into any State, Territory, or possession of the United

States for delivery or use therein of intoxicating liquors, in violation of the laws thereof, is hereby prohibited.

SECTION 3. This article shall be inoperative unless it shall have been ratified as an amendment to the Constitution by conventions in the several States, as provided in the Constitution, within seven years from the date of the submission hereof to the States by the Congress.

AMENDMENT XXII [1951]

SECTION 1. No person shall be elected to the office of the President more than twice, and no person who has held the office of President, or acted as President, for more than two years of a term to which some other person was elected president shall be elected to the office of the President more than once.

Limits a president to serving two terms

But this Article shall not apply to any person holding the office of President when this Article was proposed by the Congress, and shall not prevent any person who may be holding the office of President, or acting as President, during the term within which this Article becomes operative from holding the office of President or acting as President during the remainder of such term.

SECTION 2. This article shall be inoperative unless it shall have been ratified as an amendment to the Constitution by the legislatures of three-fourths of the several States within seven years from the date of its submission to the States by the Congress.

AMENDMENT XXIII [1961]

SECTION 1. The District constituting the seat of Government of the United States shall appoint in such manner as the Congress may direct:

*Gives Washington,
D.C., the right to
vote for president and
vice president*

A number of electors of President and Vice President equal to the whole number of Senators and Representatives in Congress to which the District would be entitled if it were a State, but in no event more than the least populous State; they shall be in addition to those appointed by the States, but they shall be considered, for the purpose of the election of President and Vice President, to be electors appointed by a State; and they shall meet in the District and perform such duties as provided by the twelfth article of amendment.

SECTION 2. The Congress shall have power to enforce this article by appropriate legislation.

AMENDMENT XXIV [1964]

*Prohibits payment of
a tax as a require-
ment to vote*

SECTION 1. The right of citizens of the United States to vote in any primary or other election for President or Vice President, for electors for President or Vice President, or for Senator or Representative in Congress, shall not be denied or abridged by the United States or any State by reason of failure to pay any poll tax or other tax.

SECTION 2. The Congress shall have power to enforce this article by appropriate legislation.

AMENDMENT XXV [1967]

SECTION 1. In case of the removal of the President from office or of his death or resignation, the Vice President shall become President.

SECTION 2. Whenever there is a vacancy in the office of the Vice President, the President shall nominate a Vice President who shall take office upon confirmation by a majority vote of both houses of Congress.

Clarifies procedure for presidential succession in case of presidential disability

SECTION 3. Whenever the President transmits to the President pro tempore of the Senate and the Speaker of the House of Representatives his written declaration that he is unable to discharge the powers and duties of his office, and until he transmits to them a written declaration to the contrary, such powers and duties shall be discharged by the Vice President as Acting President.

SECTION 4. Whenever the Vice President and a majority of either the principal officers of the executive departments, or of such other body as Congress may by law provide, transmit to the President pro tempore of the Senate and the Speaker of the House of Representatives their written declaration that the President is unable to discharge the powers and duties of his office, the Vice President shall immediately assume the powers and duties of the office as Acting President.

Thereafter, when the President transmits to the President pro tempore of the Senate and the Speaker of the House of Representatives his written declaration that no inability exists, he shall resume the powers and duties of his office unless the Vice President and a majority of either the principal officers of the executive departments, or of such other body as Congress may by law provide, transmit within four days to the president pro tempore of the Senate and the Speaker of the House of Representatives their written declaration that the President is unable to discharge the powers and duties of his office. Thereupon Congress shall decide the issue, assembling within 48 hours for that purpose if not in session. If the Congress, within 21 days after receipt of the latter written declaration, or, if Congress is not in session, within 21

days after Congress is required to assemble, deter-
mines by two-thirds vote of both houses that the
President is unable to discharge the powers and duties
of his office, the Vice President shall continue to
discharge the same as Acting President; otherwise,
the President shall resume the powers and duties of
his office.

AMENDMENT XXVI [1971]

Lowers the voting age to eighteen

SECTION 1. The right of citizens of the United
States, who are eighteen years of age or older, to vote
shall not be denied or abridged by the United States
or any state on account of age.

SECTION 2. The Congress shall have power to
enforce this article by appropriate legislation.

For Further Reading

Bonham, Barbara. *To Secure the Blessings of Liberty—The Story of Our Constitution.* Maplewood, N.J.: Hammond, 1970.

Bowen, Catherine Drinker. *Miracle at Philadelphia: The Story of the Constitutional Convention May to September 1787.* Boston: Little, Brown, 1966.

Broderick, Francis L. *The Origins of the Constitution 1776–1789.* New York: Macmillan, 1964.

Chidsey, Donald Barr. *The Birth of the Constitution: An Informal History.* New York: Crown, 1964.

Commager, Henry Steele, *The Great Constitution–A Book for Young Americans.* Indianapolis: Bobbs-Merrill, 1961.

Cooke, Donald E. *American's Great Document—The Constitution.* Maplewood, N.J.: Hammond, 1970.

Donovan, Frank Robert. *Mr. Madison's Constitution: The Story behind the Constitutional Convention.* New York: Dodd Mead, 1965.

Jensen, Merrill. *The Making of the American Constitution.* New York: Van Nostrand, 1964.

Lomask, Milton. *The Spirit of 1787: The Making of Our Constitution.* New York: Farrar Straus Giroux, 1980.

McDonald, Forrest and Ellen S., eds. *Confederation and Constitution 1781–1789.* New York: Harper and Row, 1968.

Mitchell, Broadus and Louise. *A Biography of the Constitution of the United States: Origin, Formation, Adoption, Interpretation.* New York: Oxford University Press, 1964.

Padover, Saul K. *The Living Constitution.* New York: New American Library, 1953.

Rossiter, Clinton Lawrence. *1787: The Grand Convention.* New York: Macmillan, 1966.

Smith, David G. *The Convention and the Constitution.* New York: St. Martin's Press, 1965.

Van Doren, Carl. *The Great Rehearsal: The Story of the Making and Ratifying of the Constitution of the United States.* New York: Viking Press, 1948.

Vaughan, Harold Cecil. *The Constitutional Convention 1787.* New York: Watts, 1976.

Index